What is whiter
than foam in sunlight,
moon at midnight,
snowy egret in mangrove shade?
Glacier, polar bear's paw
scooping ice hole,
cloud, tusk, egg,
eye of the vireo,
dhoti tucked between
brown thighs?
Swelled sail
on the green swell,
birch with bracelets of black,
milk in bowl
for blue-eyed cat,
parachute of the swamp mushroom,
blond shavings of pine,
dogwood's crystal face
after rain?
What is whiter?
This page before
the smudge of word.

ALSO BY MAY SWENSON

Another Animal (1954)

A Cage of Spines (1958)

To Mix with Time (1963)

Poems to Solve (1966)

Half Sun Half Sleep (1967)

Iconographs (1970)

More Poems to Solve (1971)

Windows & Stones (1972)
(translated from Tomas Tranströmer)

The Guess and Spell Coloring Book (1976)

New & Selected Things Taking Place (1978)

In Other Words (1987)

The Love Poems of May Swenson (1991)

THE
COMPLETE POEMS
TO SOLVE

May Swenson

illustrated by Christy Hale

MACMILLAN PUBLISHING COMPANY   NEW YORK

MAXWELL MACMILLAN CANADA   TORONTO

MAXWELL MACMILLAN INTERNATIONAL
NEW YORK   OXFORD   SINGAPORE   SYDNEY

"The Wonderful Pen" previously appeared in *New & Selected Things Taking Place*. All other poems in this collection, except "Whiteness," and "A Clue or Two" appeared in *Poems to Solve* and *More Poems to Solve*, published by Charles Scribner's Sons.

First edition
Printed in the United States of America

10 9 8 7 6 5 4 3 2 1

The text of this book is set in 10 pt. Meridien.
The illustrations are rendered in linocuts.

Library of Congress Cataloging-in-Publication Data
Swenson, May.
The complete poems to solve / May Swenson ; illustrated
by Christy Hale — 1st ed.
p. cm.
Includes indexes.
Summary: A selection of the author's poetry, largely dealing with nature, which challenges the reader to guess the subject of each poem or a meaning not immediately obvious.
ISBN 0-02-788725-1
1. Children's poetry, American. [1. Nature—Poetry. 2. American poetry.] I. Hale, Christy, ill. II.Title.
PS3537.W4786A6 1993   811'.54—dc20   92-26183

CONTENTS

A CLUE OR TWO   xi

SOME RIDDLE POEMS

At Breakfast   2
Was Worm   4
By Morning   5
Living Tenderly   6
Hypnotist   7
A Yellow Circle   8
An Extremity   10
Cardinal Ideograms   11
Southbound on the Freeway   13
Seven Natural Songs   14
Japanese Breakfast   15
The Surface   16
Her Management   17

FIVE CAT POEMS, FOUR BIRD POEMS, THREE SEA POEMS

Waiting for *It*   20
Cat and the Weather   21
Drawing the Cat   22
His Secret   24
Forest   26
Fountain Piece   27
Feel Like a Bird   28
The Charm Box   30
The Woods at Night   32
The Tide at Long Point   33
The Wave and the Dune   34
When You Lie Down, the Sea Stands Up   35

SOME OTHER POEMS TO FIND AND SOLVE

Green Red Brown and White   38
The Word "Beautiful"   39
Water Picture   40
The Cloud-Mobile   41
Question   42

The Wave the Flame the Cloud and the Leopard Speak
   to the Mind   43
3 Models of the Universe   44
Evolution   45
A Boy Looking at Big David   46
The Centaur   47

SPACE AND FLIGHT POEMS

After the Flight of Ranger 7   52
Orbiter 5 Shows How Earth Looks from the Moon   54
First Walk on the Moon   55
Three Jet Planes   58
Over the Field   59
Window in the Tail   60
Sleeping Overnight on the Shore   61
Of Rounds   63

WATER POEMS

At Truro   68
Out of the Sea, Early   69
Waking from a Nap on the Beach   70
Beginning to Squall   71
How Everything Happens (Based on a Study of the Wave)   72
The Stick   73
Fountains of Aix   75

WORD POEMS

To Make a Play   78
The Watch   79
Analysis of Baseball   81
The Pregnant Dream   82
MAsterMANANiMAl   84

COLOR AND SOUND POEMS

The Blindman   86
Flag of Summer   87
Colors Without Objects   89
Rain at Wildwood   90
Hearing the Wind at Night   92

Stone Gullets   93
Electronic Sound   94

CREATURE POEMS

A Pair   96
Camoufleur   97
Geometrid   98
Catbird in Redbud   99
Unconscious Came a Beauty   100
Redundant Journey   101
Motherhood   102
A Bird's Life   104
News from the Cabin   105

The Wonderful Pen   109

INDEX OF TITLES 111

INDEX OF FIRST LINES 113

ABOUT THE AUTHOR 115

A CLUE OR TWO

Each of the poems in this selection, in one way or another, is a Poem to Solve.

A characteristic of all poetry, in fact, is that more is hidden in it than in prose.

A poem, read for the first time, can offer the same pleasure as opening a wrapped box. There is the anticipation of untying an intriguing knot of words, of unloosing all their intimations like loops, of lifting out—as if from under cover—an unexpected idea or fresh sensation.

Solving a poem can be like undoing a mysterious package. The identity or significance of what's inside may be concealed or camouflaged by the dimensions or shape of its "box." Sometimes, nested within a first discovery, another may be found—which in its turn contains still another—and so on. And if then you explore all the notions in the poem, you receive the added pleasure of seeing how they relate to each other in surprising ways, while at the same time combining to create the whole design of the "box."

Having opened or solved the poem and so enjoyed its contents, you can reassemble the parts again—reimagine the whole into its original "closed" configuration. In this way you discover how the segments are shaped to interconnect.

The way that a poem is *unlike* a box is that it can enfold concepts within it that are larger than their container. Expansive elements in a poem can be packed magically into a tiny "space"—just as the word BIG, with only three letters, is *little*, yet conveys just the opposite meaning—or, conversely, the word INFINITESIMAL, which is *long*, thirteen letters, encompasses the notion of extremely small.

That is why we say of poetry that it has "magical properties"—and why we poets speak of our works as "paradoxical."

Notice how a poet's *games* are called his "works"—and how the "work" you do to solve a poem is really *play*. The impulse and motive for making a poem and for solving and enjoying a poem are quite alike: both include curiosity, alertness, joy in observation and invention.

Opening the box of a poem, looking under the wrappings and examining the various compartments can be absorbing and delightful. And, in addition to "what's in it for everybody," you may find an extra something hidden there especially for *you*—something that seems to mirror your secret feelings and thoughts, that strikes you as really true and worth keeping.

These poems were selected with the aim of presenting the direct experience of finding and recognizing, comparing and contrasting, shaping and naming, solving and enjoying—thus inviting the reader to share with the poet some of the primary pleasures of the creative act itself.

—MAY SWENSON

SOME RIDDLE POEMS

AT
BREAKFAST

Not quite
spherical
White
Oddly closed
and without a lid

A smooth miracle
here in my hand
Has it slid
from my sleeve?

The shape
of this box
keels me oval
Heels feel
its bottom
Nape knocks
its top

Seated
like a foetus
I look for
the dream-seam

What's inside?
A sun?
Off with its head
though it hasn't any
or is all head no body
a
One

Neatly
the knife scalps it
I scoop out
the braincap
soft
sweetly shuddering

Mooncream
this could be
Spoon
laps the larger
crescent
loosens a gilded
nucleus
from warm pap
A lyrical food

Opened
a seamless miracle
Ate a sun-germ
Good

WAS WORM

Was worm

swaddled in white
Now tiny queen
in sequin coat
peacockbright

drinks the wind
and feeds
on sweat of the leaves

Is little chinks
of mosaic floating
a scatter
of colored beads

Alighting pokes
with her new black wire
the saffron yokes

On silent hinges
openfolds her wings'
applauding hands
Weaned

from coddling white
to lakedeep air
to blue and green

Is queen

BY MORNING

Some for everyone
   plenty

   and more coming

Fresh   dainty   airily arriving
   everywhere at once

Transparent at first
   each faint slice
   slow   soundlessly tumbling

   then quickly thickly a gracious fleece
   will spread like youth   like wheat
   over the city

Each building will be   a hill
   all sharps made round

   dark worn noisy narrows made still
   wide   flat   clean   spaces

Streets will be   fields
   cars be   fumbling sheep

A deep bright harvest will be seeded
   in a night

By morning we'll be   children
   feeding on manna

   a new loaf on every doorsill

LIVING TENDERLY

My body a rounded stone
with a pattern of smooth seams.
My head a short snake,
retractive, projective.
My legs come out of their sleeves
or shrink within,
and so does my chin.
My eyelids are quick clamps.

My back is my roof.
I am always at home.
I travel where my house walks.
It is a smooth stone.
It floats within the lake,
or rests in the dust.
My flesh lives tenderly
inside its bone.

HYPNOTIST

His lair framed beneath the clock,
a red-haired beast hypnotic in the room
glazes our eyes and draws us close
with delicious snarls and flickers of his claws.
We stir our teacups and our wishes feast
on his cruelty.

Throw the Christian chairs to him,
a wild child in us cries.
Or let us be Daniel bared
to that seething maze his mane.
Loops of his fur graze the sill
where the clock's face looks scared.

Comfort-ensnared and languorous
our unused daring, roused, resembles him
fettered on the hearth's stage
behind the iron dogs.
He's the red locks of the sun
brought home to a cage.

Hunched before his flaring shape
we stir our teacups.
We wish he would escape
and loosen in ourselves the terrible.
But only his reflection pounces
on the parquet and the stair.

A YELLOW
CIRCLE

A green
string
is fastened
to the earth

at its apex
a yellow
circle

of silky
superimposed
spokes
The sun
is its mother

Later
the string
is taller
The circle
is white

an aureole
of evanescent
hairs
the wind
makes breathe

Later still
it is altered
the green
string
is thicker

the white
circle
bald
on one side

It is a half
circle
the wind lifts away

AN EXTREMITY

Roused from napping in my lap,
this nimble animal or five-legged star
parts its limbs sprat-wide.
See where they glide to focus at their base as spokes of a
      harp.
Blunt and fat the first,
sharp-tipped tapping the next,
the third authentic and the fourth shy,
the least, a runt, begs pardon for his stature. Why,
they're separate beasts I see, and not one beast with legs!

Or a family of dolls.
You could dress the tallest as a boy.
Already his sister wears a silver belt.
That's a toy-baby by her curled, if you put a bonnet on it.
Here's agile-joint, the pointed, the smart wife.
Square-head, short and papa-perfect, sits apart
in dignity, a wart at knuckle.

Turned over open, inner skin is vellum. Here's a map.
Five islands spread from the mainland in the fist.
Seen flat, it's a plain.
Forked rivers thread to the wrist,
or call them roads, the rosy pattern sprawled in an M.
Forests are stitched with prick-hatched pine-tree criss-
      marks.
Whorled lines are ploughed land. And
ending each pentacle beach are U-bands of sea-rippled
      sand.

Left one looked at, right one writes:
Star, Harp, Beast, Family of Five,
Map laid live in my lap.
Clapped together the two arrive, are stated,
the poem made, extremities mated.

CARDINAL IDEOGRAMS

0   A mouth.   Can blow or breathe,
    be funnel, or Hello.

1   A grass blade or a cut.

2   A question seated.   And a proud
    bird's neck.

3   Shallow mitten for two-fingered hand.

4   Three-cornered hut
    on one stilt.   Sometimes built
    so the roof gapes.

5   A policeman.   Polite.
    Wearing visored cap.

6   O unrolling,
    tape of ambiguous length
    on which is written the mystery
    of everything curly.

7   A step,
    detached from its stair.

8   The universe in diagram:
    A cosmic hourglass.
    (Note enigmatic shape,
    absence of any valve of origin,
    how end overlaps beginning.)
    Unknotted like a shoelace
    and whipped back and forth,
    can serve as a model of time.

9   Lorgnette for the right eye.
In England or if you are Alice
the stem is on the left.

10   A grass blade or a cut
companioned by a mouth.
Open? Open. Shut? Shut.

SOUTHBOUND ON THE FREEWAY

A tourist came in from Orbitville,
parked in the air, and said:

The creatures of this star
are made of metal and glass.

Through the transparent parts
you can see their guts.

Their feet are round and roll
on diagrams—or long

measuring tapes—dark
with white lines.

They have four eyes.
The two in the back are red.

Sometimes you can see a 5-eyed
one, with a red eye turning

on the top of his head.
He must be special—

the others respect him,
and go slow,

when he passes, winding
among them from behind.

They all hiss as they glide,
like inches, down the marked

tapes. Those soft shapes,
shadowy inside

the hard bodies—are they
their guts or their brains?

SEVEN NATURAL SONGS

1   Awoke and stretched in all the bodies
     lofted on sinewy air. Clipped out
     beak-shaped cries and skinned the mist
     from the morning.

2   Stood wooden, wiggled in earth way under.
     A toenail scraped a mammoth's tusk.
     Jounced and jittered all these lippy leaves.

3   Slicked along meddling with rocks. Tore
     their ears off gradually. Sparkling made
     them hop and holler down a slate-cold throat.

4   Humped up, sucked in all my thongs
     belly-deep to the roaring core. Recoiled
     for a big yellow bloom. Burst and hurled
     wide open pods of light everywhere.

5   Loosened and looled elongate in hammocks
     of blue. Evasive of shape and the eggshell's
     curve. Without taint or tint or substance
     dissolved in fleecy sloth.

6   Pricked up out of each pore, urgent, ambitious,
     itching to be even. Scurried and spread
     so all is kept level. Forever unfinished
     my mass fernal mystery. Ants read its roots,
     tell its juices to sand.

7   Once cloud, now all memory my motion.
     Amorphous creeping slow as sleep to a full
     black gulping flood. The small five-fingered
     blot enlarged beyond identity. Heavy, unslaked,
     still hunting form. The hiding place,
     the necessary horror.

1 Birds 2 Tree 3 Waterfall 4 Sun
5 Clouds 6 Grass 7 Shadow

JAPANESE BREAKFAST

The table of the pool is set.
Each cup quivers by a plate.

Some are filled with tea of sun,
some have pinks of liquor in;

some, thick and white, look upside down
as if put out to dry,

or not to use till morning
pours a thinner cream.

Lying out lopsided,
all the plates are green.

Immaculate as in Japan
the food is only dew,

but fountain-flounce, the table cloth,
shows a rainbow stain.

Some black-nosed goldfish passing through
on their way to shade

nudge the rocking saucers.
A wet ceramic toad,

descending stairs of moss
to breakfast on an insect,

upsets the level table top
but leaves the cups intact.

THE SURFACE

First I saw the surface,
then I saw it flow,
then I saw the underneath.

In gradual light below
I saw a kind of room,
the ceiling was a veil,

a shape swam there
slow, opaque and pale.
I saw enter by a shifting corridor

other blunt bodies
that sank toward the floor.
I tried to follow deeper

with my avid eye.
Something changed the focus:
I saw the sky,

a glass between inverted trees.
Then I saw my face.
I looked until a cloud

flowed over that place.
Now I saw the surface
broad to its rim,

here gleaming, there opaque
far out, flat and dim.
Then I saw it was an Eye:

I saw the Wink that slid
from underneath the surface
before it closed its lid.

HER MANAGEMENT

She does not place, relate, or name
the objects of her hall,
nor bother to repair her ceiling,
sweep her floor, or paint a wall
symmetrical with mountains.

Cylindrical, her tent
is pitched of ocean on one side
and—rakish accident—
forest on the other;
granular, her rug

of many marbles, or of roots,
or needles, or a bog—
outrageous in its pattern.
The furniture is pine
and oak and birch and beech and elm;

the water couch is fine.
Mottled clouds, and lightning rifts,
leaking stars and whole
gushing moons despoil her roof.
Contemptuous of control,

she lets a furnace burn all day,
she lets the winds be wild.
Broken, rotting, shambled things
lie where they like, are piled
on the same tables with her sweets,

her fruits, and scented stuffs.
Her management is beauty.
Of careless silks and roughs,
rumpled rocks, the straightest rain,
blizzards, roses, crows,

April lambs and graveyards,
she *chances* to compose
a rich and sloven manor.
Her prosperous tapestries
are too effusive in design

for our analyses—
we, who through her textures move,
we specks upon her glass,
who try to place, relate and name
all things within her mass.

FIVE CAT POEMS,
FOUR BIRD POEMS,
THREE SEA POEMS

WAITING FOR *It*

My cat jumps to the window sill
and sits there still as a jug.
He's waiting for me, but I cannot be
coming, for I am in the room.

His snout, a gloomy V of patience,
pokes out into the sun.
The funnels of his ears expect
to be poured full of my footsteps.

It, the electric moment, a sweet
mouse, will appear; at his gray
eye's edge I'll be coming home
if he sits on the window-ledge.

It is here, I say, and call him
to my lap. Not a hair
in the gap of his ear moves.
His clay gaze stays steady.

That solemn snout says: *It*
is what is about to happen, not
what is already here.

CAT AND THE WEATHER

Cat takes a look at the weather.
Snow.
Puts a paw on the sill.
His perch is piled, is a pillow.

Shape of his pad appears.
Will it dig? No.
Not like sand.
Like his fur almost.

But licked, not liked.
Too cold.
Insects are flying, fainting down.
He'll try

to bat one against the pane.
They have no body and no buzz.
And now his feet are wet;
it's a puzzle.

Shakes each leg,
then shakes his skin
to get the white flies off.
Looks for his tail,

tells it to come on in
by the radiator.
World's turned queer
somehow. All white,

no smell. Well, here
inside it's still familiar.
He'll go to sleep until
it puts itself right.

DRAWING THE CAT

Makes a platform for himself:
forepaws bent under his chest,
slot-eyes shut in a corniced head,
haunches high like a wing chair,
hindlegs parallel, a sled.

As if on water, low afloat
like a wooden duck: a bundle not
apt to be tipped, so symmetrized
on hidden keel of tail he rides
squat, arrested, glazed.

Lying flat, a violin:
hips are splayed, head and chin
sunk on paws, stem straight out
from the arched root
at the clef-curve of the thighs.

Wakes: the head ball rises.
Claws sprawl. Wires
go taut, make a wicket of his spine.
He humps erect, with scimitar yawn
of hooks and needles porcupine.

Sits, solid as a doorstop,
tail-encircled, tip laid on his toes,
ear-tabs stiff, gooseberry eyes
full, unblinking, sourly wise.
In outline: a demijohn with a pewter look.

Swivels, bends a muscled neck:
petal-of-tulip-tongue slicks

the brushpoint of his tail to black,
then smooths each glossy epaulette
with assiduous sponge.

Whistle him into a canter
into the kitchen: tail hooked aside,
ears at the ready. Elegant copy
of carrousel pony—
eyes bright as money.

HIS SECRET

I took my cat apart
to see what made him purr.
Like an electric clock
or like the snore

of a warming kettle,
something fizzed and sizzled in him.
Was he a soft car,
the engine bubbling sound?

Was there a wire beneath his fur,
or humming throttle?
I undid his throat.
Within was no stir.

I opened up his chest
as though it were a door:
no whisk or rattle there.
I lifted off his skull:

no hiss or murmur.
I halved his little belly
but found no gear,
no cause for static.

So I replaced his lid,
laced his little gut.
His heart into his vest I slid
and buttoned up his throat.

His tail rose to a rod
and beckoned to the air.
Some voltage made him vibrate
warmer than before.

Whiskers and a tail:
perhaps they caught
some radar code
emitted as a pip, a dot-and-dash

of woolen sound.
My cat a kind of tuning-fork?—
amplifier?—telegraph?—
doing secret signal work?

His eyes elliptic tubes:
there's a message in his stare.
I stroke him
but cannot find the dial.

FOREST

The pines, aggressive as erect tails of cats,
bob their tips when the wind freshens.

An alert breath like purring stirs below,
where I move timid over humps of hair,

crisp, shadow-brindled, heaving as if
exhilarated muscular backs felt

the wisps of my walking. Looking to sky,
glaring then closing between the slow

lashes of boughs, I feel observed:
up high are oblong eyes that know,

as their slits of green light
expand, squeeze shut, expand,

that I stand here. Suddenly I go,
flick-eyed, hurrying over fur

needles that whisper as if they weren't dead.
My neck-hairs rise. The feline forest grins

behind me. Is it about to follow?
Which way out through all these whiskered yawns?

FOUNTAIN PIECE

A bird
   is perched
      upon a wing

     The wing
   is stone
The bird
is real

A drapery
   falls about this form
     The form is stone
       The dress is rain

      The pigeon preens his own
    and does not know
   he sits upon a wing
   The angel does not feel
  a relative among her large
  feathers stretch
  and take his span
  in charge
  and leave her there
with her cold
wings that cannot fold
while his fan
in air.

The fountain raining
  wets the stone
    but does not know it dresses
    an angel in its tresses

    Her stone cheek smiles
   and does not care
  that real tears
flow there

FEEL LIKE A BIRD

feel like A Bird
understand
he has no hand

instead A Wing
close-lapped
mysterious thing

in sleeveless coat
he halves The Air
skipping there
like water-licked boat

lands on star-toes
finger-beak in
feather-pocket
finds no coin

in neat head like
seeds in A Quartered
Apple eyes join
sniping at opposites
stereoscope The Scene
Before

close to floor giddy
no arms to fling
A Third Sail
spreads for calm
his tail

hand better
than A Wing?
to gather A Heap
to count
to clasp A Mate?

or leap
lone-free and mount
on muffled shoulders
to span A Fate?

THE CHARM BOX

As if the knob
perhaps of porcelain
of a small calliope
were turned around twice

then a hush
while the memory
of the dainty fragment
is listened to by the box itself

the hermit thrush
that plain instrument
not seeming precious
twice releases its throb

This double jewel
this melodious jangle
is all there's in it
One expects the knob to spin

and in a rush
a long-looped ornament of every color
to dangle down the air
A spoke in there

is not broken
That stunted quirk
repeated
with attention to the silence in between

is the amulet
that makes the charm box work
The hermit thrush
refuses to be luscious

to elaborate to entangle
to interpret
or even to declare a goal
Only the strict reiteration of a rarity

from this small calliope
until it is convinced its bare
beginning is the end
and the whole

THE WOODS AT NIGHT

The binocular owl,
fastened to a limb
like a lantern
all night long,

sees where all
the other birds sleep:
towhee under leaves,
titmouse deep

in a twighouse,
sapsucker gripped
to a knothole lip,
redwing in the reeds,

swallow in the willow,
flicker in the oak—
but cannot see poor
whippoorwill

under the hill
in deadbrush nest,
who's awake, too—
with stricken eye

flayed by the moon
her brindled breast
repeats, repeats, repeats its plea
for cruelty.

THE TIDE AT LONG POINT

The sea comes up and the sun goes over
   The sea goes out and the sun falls
The stubby shadow of the lighthouse pales
   stretches to a finger and inches east
The wind lifts from off the sea
   and curries and curries the manes of the dunes
The pipers and the terns skate over
   tweaking the air with their talk
In sky clean as a cat-licked dish
   clouds are sandbars bared by ebbing blue

The hourglass is reversed

The sea comes up and the moon peers over
   The sea goes out and the moon swells
The shadow of the lighthouse thick as a boot
   is swiped by a whiskered beam
The wind licks at the jetty stones
   The pipers and terns hunch on the spit
hiding their necks and stilted feet
   The sky has caught a netful of stars
The moon is a dory trolling them in

The hourglass is reversed

The sea comes up and the moon tips under
   The sea goes out and the sun looms
The sun is a schooner making for harbor
   Shallops of cloud are adrift in the west
The wind gallops the waves to a lather
   and lashes the grass that shines on the dunes
The lighthouse looks at its twin in the water
   The pipers and terns preen on its brow

THE WAVE AND THE DUNE

The wave-shaped dune is still.
Its curve does not break,
though it looks as if it will,

like the head of the dune-
shaped wave advancing,
its ridge strewn

with white shards flaking.
A sand-faced image of the wave
is always in the making.

Opposite the sea's rough glass
cove, the sand's smooth-whittled cave
under the brow of grass

is sunny and still. Rushing
to place its replica
on the shore, the sea is pushing

sketches of itself
incessantly into the foreground.
All the models smash upon the shelf,

but, grain by grain, the creeping sand
reërects their profiles
and makes them stand.

WHEN YOU LIE DOWN,
THE SEA STANDS UP

Thick twisted cables
   of bottle glass at the base,
gunbarrel-blue higher up,
 are quickly being braided and stretched
their condition molten,
      their surface cold.
Or they are the long smooth logs of a pile
   being built from the top down.
The trunks of greatest girth
     arrive at the bottom
with silver rips and ridges in their bark.
    There is a wall in motion
like a lathe of light
    and dark galvanic blue
layers which are twirling,
  extending beyond your eye-points.
You cannot see their ends.

  Watch the topmost thinnest strand,
too taut to quiver:
   Above is a calcimined ceiling,
heliotrope... steady...
   delicate as for a bedroom.

SOME OTHER POEMS
TO FIND AND SOLVE

GREEN RED BROWN
AND WHITE

Bit an apple on its red
side. Smelled like snow.
Between white halves broken open,
brown winks slept in sockets of green.

Stroked a birch white as a thigh,
scar-flecked, smooth as the neck
of a horse. On mossy pallets green
the pines dropped down
their perfect carvings brown.

Lost in the hairy wood,
followed berries red
to the fork. Had to choose
between green and green. High

in a sunwhite dome a brown bird
sneezed. Took the path least likely
and it led me home. For

each path leads both out and in.
I come while going. No to and from.
There is only here. And here
is as well as there. Wherever
I am led I move within the care
of the season,
hidden in the creases of her skirts
of green or brown or beaded red.

And when they are white,
I am not lost. I am not lost then,
only covered for the night.

THE WORD "BEAUTIFUL"

Long, glossy caterpillar
with softest feet
of audible and inaudible vowels;

dewberry head so black
it's silver;
nippered lip, and fluent rump;

who moves by the T
at his tifted middle,
a little locomotive hump.

His ripple is felt
by the palm ashamed,
and we are loath to name him;

hairs of his back
a halo's paint
we daren't put round objects any more.

He's tainted,
doomed to sloth, like those
other lunar insects such

as Velvet
that we must not touch,
or Rose, or Gold.

His destiny—
a myth or moth—still glows
inside the skull,

although his creep is blue,
the untrusted phosphor
of our sleep.

WATER PICTURE

In the pond in the park
all things are doubled:
Long buildings hang and
wriggle gently. Chimneys
are bent legs bouncing
on clouds below. A flag
wags like a fishhook
down there in the sky.

The arched stone bridge
is an eye, with underlid
in the water. In its lens
dip crinkled heads with hats
that don't fall off. Dogs go by,
barking on their backs.
A baby, taken to feed the
ducks, dangles upside-down,
a pink balloon for a buoy.

Treetops deploy a haze of
cherry bloom for roots,
where birds coast belly-up
in the glass bowl of a hill;
from its bottom a bunch
of peanut-munching children
is suspended by their
sneakers, waveringly.

A swan, with twin necks
forming the figure three,
steers between two dimpled
towers doubled. Fondly
hissing, she kisses herself,
and all the scene is troubled:
water-windows splinter,
tree-limbs tangle, the bridge
folds like a fan.

THE CLOUD-MOBILE

Above my face is a map
where continents form and fade.
Blue countries, made
on a white sea, are erased;
white countries are traced
on a blue sea.

It is a map that moves
faster than real
but so slow;
only my watching proves
that island has being,
or that bay.

It is a model of time;
mountains are wearing away,
coasts cracking, the ocean
spills over, then new
hills heap into view
with river-cuts of blue between them.

It is a map of change:
this is the way things are
with a stone or a star.
This is the way things go,
hard or soft,
swift or slow.

QUESTION

Body my house
my horse my hound
what will I do
when you are fallen

Where will I sleep
How will I ride
What will I hunt

Where can I go
without my mount
all eager and quick
How will I know
in thicket ahead
is danger or treasure
when Body my good
bright dog is dead

How will it be
to lie in the sky
without roof or door
and wind for an eye

With cloud for shift
how will I hide?

THE WAVE THE FLAME THE CLOUD AND THE LEOPARD SPEAK TO THE MIND

Watch and watch and follow me
I am all green mimicry
        In my manyness you see
what engenders my beauty

        Dancer red and gold with greed
I am that which does not bleed
    On my rising breath be carried
Twine with me and so be freed

    Ride with me and hold my mane
I am chimaera the skein
        of everchange that's lily-lain
above the steady mountain

            Go the circle of my cage
I own nothing but my rage
    the black and white of the savage
This singleness may you assuage

3 MODELS OF THE UNIVERSE

1   At moment X
the universe began.
It began at point X.
Since then,
through The Hole in a Nozzle,
stars have spewed. An
inexhaustible gush
populates the void forever.

2   The universe was there
before time ran.
A grain
slipped in the glass:
the past began.
The Container
of the Stars expands;
the sand
of matter multiplies forever.

3   From zero radius
to a certain span,
the universe, A Large Lung
specked with stars,
inhales time
until, turgent, it can
hold no more,
and collapses. Then
space breathes, and inhales again,
and breathes again: Forever.

EVOLUTION

the stone	how i Yearn
would like to be	for the lion
Alive like me	in his den
	though he spurn
the rooted tree	the touch of men
longs to be Free	
	the longing
the mute beast	that I know
envies my fate	is in the Stone also
Articulate	it must be
	the same that rises
on this Ball	in the Tree
half dark half light	the longing
i walk Upright	in the Lion's call
i lie Prone	speaks for all
within the night	
	oh to Endure
beautiful each Shape	like the stone
to see	sufficient to itself alone
wonderful each Thing	
to name	or Reincarnate
here a stone	like the tree
there a tree	be born each spring
here a River	to greenery
there a Flame	
	or like the lion
marvelous to Stroke	without law
the patient beasts	to roam the Wild
within their yoke	on velvet paw
but if walking i meet	during.my.delight
a Creature like me	with Him
on the street	
two-legged	an Evolution strange
with human face	two Tongues touch
to recognize is to Embrace	exchange
	a Feast unknown
wonders pale	to stone
beauties dim	or tree or beast

A BOY LOOKING AT BIG DAVID

I'm touching his toe.
I know I'll be brave after this.
His toenail wide as my hand,
I have to stand tall to reach it.

The big loose hand with the rock in it
by his thigh
is high above my head. The vein
from wrist to thumb, a blue strain in the marble.

As if it had natural anatomy all its own
inside it.
Somebody skinned off the top stone,
and there He stands.

I'd like to climb up there on that slippery Hip,
shinny up to the Shoulder
the other side of that thumping Neck,
and lie in the ledge on the collar-bone,

by the sling.
In that cool place
I'd stare-worship that big, full-lipped,
frown-browned, far-eyed, I-dare-you-Face.

I'd like to live on that David for a while,
get to know
how to be immortal like Him.
But I can only reach his Toe—

broad, poking over the edge of the stand.
So cool…
Maybe, marble Him,
he likes the warm of my hand?

THE CENTAUR

The summer that I was ten—
Can it be there was only one
summer that I was ten? It must

have been a long one then—
each day I'd go out to choose
a fresh horse from my stable

which was a willow grove
down by the old canal.
I'd go on my two bare feet.

But when, with my brother's jack-knife,
I had cut me a long limber horse
with a good thick knob for a head,

and peeled him slick and clean
except a few leaves for the tail,
and cinched my brother's belt

around his head for a rein,
I'd straddle and canter him fast
up the grass bank to the path,

trot along in the lovely dust
that talcumed over his hoofs,
hiding my toes, and turning

his feet to swift half-moons.
The willow knob with the strap
jouncing between my thighs

was the pommel and yet the poll
of my nickering pony's head.
My head and my neck were mine,

yet they were shaped like a horse.
My hair flopped to the side
like the mane of a horse in the wind.

My forelock swung in my eyes,
my neck arched and I snorted.
I shied and skittered and reared,

stopped and raised my knees,
pawed at the ground and quivered.
My teeth bared as we wheeled

and swished through the dust again.
I was the horse and the rider,
and the leather I slapped to his rump

spanked my own behind.
Doubled, my two hoofs beat
a gallop along the bank,

the wind twanged in my mane,
my mouth squared to the bit.
And yet I sat on my steed

quiet, negligent riding,
my toes standing the stirrups,
my thighs hugging his ribs.

At a walk we drew up to the porch.
I tethered him to a paling.
Dismounting, I smoothed my skirt

and entered the dusky hall.
My feet on the clean linoleum
left ghostly toes in the hall.

Where have you been? said my mother.
Been riding, I said from the sink,
and filled me a glass of water.

What's that in your pocket? she said.
Just my knife. It weighted my pocket
and stretched my dress awry.

Go tie back your hair, said my mother,
and *Why is your mouth all green?*
*Rob Roy, he pulled some clover
as we crossed the field*, I told her.

SPACE AND FLIGHT POEMS

AFTER THE FLIGHT OF RANGER 7

Moon, old fossil,
to be scrubbed

and studied like
a turtle's stomach,

prodded over
on your back,

invulnerable hump
that stumped us,

pincers prepare to
pick your secrets,

bludgeons of light
to force your seams.

Old fossil, glistening
in the continuous rain

of meteorites
blown to you from

between the stars,
stilt feet mobilize

to alight upon you,
ticking feelers

determine your fissures,
to impact a pest

of electric eggs
in the cracks

of your cold
volcanoes. Tycho,

Copernicus, Kepler,
look for geysers,

strange abrasions,
zodiacal wounds.

ORBITER 5 SHOWS
HOW EARTH LOOKS FROM THE MOON

There's a woman in the earth, sitting on
her heels. You see her from the back, in three-
quarter profile. She has a flowing pigtail. She's
holding something
in her right hand—some holy jug. Her left arm is thinner,
in a gesture like a dancer. She's the Indian Ocean. Asia is
light swirling up out of her vessel. Her pigtail points to Europe
and her dancer's arm is the Suez Canal. She is a woman
in a square kimono,
bare feet tucked beneath the tip of Africa. Her tail of long hair is
the Arabian Peninsula.   A woman in the earth.

                                              A man in the moon

Note: A telephoto of the earth, taken from above the moon by Lunar
Orbiter 5 (printed in *The New York Times* August 14, 1967) appeared to
show the shadow-image of "a woman in a square Kimono" between the
shapes of the continents. The title is the headline over the photo.

FIRST WALK ON THE MOON

Ahead, the sun's face in a flaring hood,
was wearing the moon, a mask of shadow
that stood between. Cloudy earth
waned, gibbous, while our target grew:
an occult bloom, until it lay beneath
the fabricated insect we flew. Pitched
out of orbit we yawed in, to impact
softly on that circle.

                  Not "ground"
the footpads found for traction.
So far, we haven't the name.
So call it "terrain," pitted and pocked
to the round horizon (which looked
too near): a slope of rubble where
protuberant cones, dish-shaped hollows,
great sockets glared, half blind
with shadow, and smaller sucked-in folds
squinted, like blowholes on a scape
of whales.

                Rigid and pneumatic, we
emerged, white twin uniforms on the dark
"mare," our heads transparent spheres,
the outer visors gold. The light was
glacier bright, our shadows long,
thin fissures, of "ink." We felt neither
hot nor cold.

                 Our boot cleats sank
into "grit, something like glass,"
but sticky. Our tracks remain
on what was virgin "soil." But that's
not the name.

There was no air there,
no motion, no sound outside our heads.
We brought what we breathed
on our backs: the square papooses we
carried were our life sacks. We spoke
in numbers, fed the ratatattat of data
to amplified earth. We saw no spore
that any had stepped before us. Not
a thing has been born here, and nothing
has died, we thought.

We had practiced
to walk, but we toddled (with caution,
lest ambition make us fall
to our knees on that alien "floor.")
We touched nothing with bare hands.
Our gauntlets lugged the cases of gear,
deployed our probes and emblems,
set them prudently near the insect liftoff
station, with its flimsy ladder to home.

All day it was night, the sky black
vacuum, though the strobe of the low sun
smote ferocious on that "loam."
We could not stoop, but scooped up
"clods" of the clinging "dust," that flowed
and glinted black, like "graphite."
So, floating while trotting, hoping not
to stub our toe, we chose and catalogued
unearthly "rocks." These we stowed.

And all night it was day, you could say,
with cloud-cuddled earth in the zenith,
a ghost moon that swivelled. The stars
were all displaced, or else were not
the ones we knew. Maneuvering by numbers
copied from head to head, we surveyed
our vacant outpost. Was it a "petrified
sea bed," inert "volcanic desert," or
crust over quivering "magma," that might
quake?

        It was possible to stand there.
And we planted a cloth "flower":
our country colors we rigged to blow
in the non-wind. We could not lift
our arms eye-high (they might deflate)
but our camera was a pistol, the trigger
built into the grip, and we took each
other's pictures, shooting from the hip.
Then bounced and loped euphoric,
enjoying our small weight.

            Our flash
eclipsed the sun at takeoff. We left our
insect belly "grounded," and levitated,
standing in its head. The dark dents
of our boots, unable to erode, mark how
we came: two white mechanic knights,
the first, to make tracks in some kind
of "sand." The footpads found it solid, so
we "landed." But that's not the right name.

THREE JET PLANES

Three jet planes skip above the roofs
   through a tri-square of blue
   tatooed by TV crossbars
   that lean in cryptic concert in their wake

Like skaters on a lake
   combined to a perfect arrowhead up there
   they sever space with bloodless speed
   and are gone without a clue
   but a tiny bead the eye can scarcely find
   leaving behind
   where they first burst into blue
   the invisible boiling wind of sound

As horsemen used to do
As horsemen used to gallop through
   a hamlet on hunting morn
   and heads and arms were thrust
   through windows
   leaving behind them the torn
   shriek of the hound
   and their wrestling dust

Above the roofs three jet planes
   leave their hoofs of violence on naïve ground

OVER THE FIELD

They have
a certain
beauty, those
wheeled
fish, when over the field, steel fins stiff
out from
their sides
they grope,

and then
through cloud
slice
silver snouts,
and climb,
trailing glamorous veils like slime.

Their long abdomens cannot curve, but
arrogant cut
blue, power
enflaming

their gills.
They claim
that sea where no fish swam until they flew
to minnow it
with their
metal.

The inflexible bellies carry, like roe,
Jonahs
sitting
row on row.
I sit by the
fin, in

one of those whale-big, wheeled fish, while
several silver
minnows line
up, rolling
the runway way
below.

WINDOW IN THE TAIL

Nap of cloud, as thick as stuffing
tight packed for a mattress ticking,

pickaninny kinked and puffed
and white as kid-sheared belly ruff,

is the floor and is the ceiling
over which we're keeled and sailing,

on flat pinion—not of feather—
but slatted aluminum or other

metal maneuverable
by ample ramps that bevel

up, or slide out wide
and glide

our carriage level.
Over fur of cloud we travel.

SLEEPING OVERNIGHT ON THE SHORE

Earth turns
          one cheek to the sun
while the other tips
          its crags and dimples into shadow.
We say sun comes up,
          goes down,
but it is our planet's incline
          on its shy invisible neck.
The smooth skin of the sea,
          the bearded buttes of the land
blush orange,
          we say it is day.
Then earth in its turning
          slips half of itself away
from the ever burning.
          Night's frown
smirches earth's face,
          by those hours marked older.
It is dark, we say.
          But night is a fiction
hollowed at the back of our ball,
          when from its obverse side
a cone of self-thrown shade
          evades the shining,
and black and gray
          the cinema of dreams streams through
our sandgrain skulls
          lit by our moon's outlining.

Intermittent moon
          that we say climbs
or sets, circles only.
          Earth flicks it past its shoulder.
It tugs at the teats of the sea.
          And sky
is neither high
          nor is earth low.

There is no dark
            but distance
between stars.
            No dawn,
for it is always day
            on Gas Mountain, on the sun—
and horizon's edge
            the frame of our eye.

Cool sand on which we lie
            and watch the gray waves
clasp, unclasp
            a restless froth of light,
silver saliva of the sucking moon—
            whose sun is earth
who's moon to the sun—
            To think this shore,
each lit grain plain
            in the foot-shaped concaves
heeled with shadow,
            is pock or pocket
on an aging pin
            that juggler sun once threw,
made twirl among
            those other blazing objects out
around its crown.
            And from that single toss
the Nine still tumble—
            swung in a carousel of staring light,
where each rides ringleted
            by its pebble-moons—
white lumps of light
            that are never to alight,
for there is no down.

OF ROUNDS

MOON
  round
    goes around while going around a
          round
           EARTH.
EARTH
  round
    with MOON
      round
       going around while going around,
goes around while going around a
       round
        SUN.
SUN
  round
    with EARTH
      round
       with MOON
        round
         going around while going
around, and MERCURY
      round
     and VENUS
       round
        going around while
going around, and MARS
      round
     with two MOONS
        round
        round
         going around
while going around, and JUPITER
      round
       with fifteen MOONS
          round
          round
          round
          round
          round
          round
          round

                                        round
                                        round
                                        round
                                        round
                                        round
                                        round
                                        round
                                        round
going around while going around, and SATURN
                                    round
                                        with fifteen
MOONS
        round
        round
        round
        round
        round
        round
        round
        round
        round
        round
        round
        round
        round
        round
        round
                going around while going around, and URANUS
                                            round
with five MOONS
                round
                round
                round
                round
                round
                        going around while going around, and NEPTUNE
round
        with two MOONS
                    round
                    round
                        going around while going around, and

PLUTO

    round

       going around while going around, goes around while
going around

     A

    OF ROUNDS

           Round

WATER POEMS

AT TRURO

The sea is unfolding scrolls
and rolling them up again.
It is an ancient diary

the waves are murmuring.
The words are white curls,
great capitals are seen

on the wrinkled swells.
Repeated rhythmically
it seems to me I read

my own biography.
Once I was a sea bird.
With beak a sharp pen,

I drew my signature on air.
There is a chapter when,
a crab, I slowly scratched

my name on a sandy page,
and once, a coral, wrote
a record of my age

on the wall of a water-grotto.
When I was a sea worm
I never saw the sun,

but flowed, a salty germ,
in the bloodstream of the sea.
There I left an alphabet

but it grew dim to me.
Something caught me in its net,
took me from the deep

book of the ocean, weaned me,
put fin and wing to sleep,
made me stand and made me

face the sun's dry eye.
On the shore of intellect
I forgot how to fly

above the wave, below it.
When I touched my foot
to land's thick back,

it stuck like stem or root.
In brightness I lost track
of my underworld

of ultraviolet wisdom.
My fiery head furled
up its cool kingdom

and put night away.
The sea is unfolding scrolls,
and rolling them up.

As if the sun were blind
again I feel the suck
of the sea's dark mind.

OUT OF THE SEA, EARLY

A bloody
egg yolk. A burnt hole
spreading in a sheet. An en-
raged rose threatening to bloom.
A furnace hatchway opening, roaring.
A globular bladder filling with immense
juice. I start to scream. A red hydrocepha-
lic head is born, teetering on the stump of
its neck. When it separates, it leaks rasp-
berry from the horizon down the wide esca-
lator. The cold blue boiling waves cannot
scour out that band, that broadens, slid-
ing toward me up the wet sand slope. The
fox-hair grows, grows thicker on the
upfloating head. By six o'clock,
diffused to ordinary gold,
it exposes each silk thread and rumple in the carpet.

WAKING FROM A NAP ON THE BEACH

Sounds like big
rashers of bacon frying.
I look up from where I'm lying
expecting to see stripes

red and white. My eyes drop shut,
stunned by the sun.
Now the foam is flame, the long
troughs charcoal, but

still it chuckles and sizzles, it
burns and burns, it never gets done.
The sea is that
fat.

BEGINNING TO SQUALL

A Buoy like a man in a red sou'wester
is uP to the toP of its Boots in the water
   leaning to warn a Blue Boat

     that, BoBBing and shrugging, is nodding "No,"
      till a strong wave comes and it shivers "Yes."
       The white and the green Boats are quiBBling, too.
       What is it they don't want to do?

The Bay goes on Bouncing anchor floats,
their colors tennis and tangerine.
Two ruffled gulls laughing are laughing gulls,
  a finial Pair on the gray Pilings.

     Now the Boats are Buttoning slickers on
      which resemBle little tents.
       The Buoy is jumPing uP and down
        showing a Black Belt stenciled "1."

A yellow Boat's last to lower sail
to wraP like a Bandage around the Boom.
   Blades are sharPening in the water
      that Brightens while the sky goes duller.

HOW EVERYTHING HAPPENS
(Based on a Study of the Wave)

happen.

to

up

stacking

is

something

When nothing is happening

When it happens

something

pulls

back

not

to

happen.

When   has happened.

pulling back   stacking up

happens

has happened   stacks up.

When it   something   nothing

pulls back while

Then nothing is happening.

happens.

and

forward

pushes

up

stacks

something

Then

72

THE STICK

The stick is subject to the waves. The waves are subject to
the sea. The sea is subject to its frame. And that
is fixed, or seems to be.

What is it that the stick can do? Can tell the sky, "I
dip, I float. When a wave runs under me, I pretend
I am a boat. And the steersman and
the crew, and the cargo, compass, map. With
a notion of the shore,
I carry all within my lap."

And when a wave runs over it, what is it that the
stick decides? "From your bottom,
cruel sea, you have torn me with your
tides. I am a sliver from some boat, once
swallowed to its water-deep. Why
am I shifted, broken, lost? Let me down, my
rest to keep."

The sea is subject to its frame.
The waves are subject to the sea. The
stick is subject to the waves.
Or does it only seem to be?

What if the stick be washed ashore,
and, gnawed by wind, scoured
by sand, be taken up with other
sticks, into a hand? On some
predicated day, here is what
the stick might say:

"Inside my border, a green
sea flows, that while it
flows is still. A white
wall is around me,
where I am fixed by
someone's will,
who made my shape
into a frame,
and in
this corner
drew
his
name."

FOUNTAINS OF AIX

Beards of   water
some of them have.
Others are blowing whistles of   water.
Faces astonished that constant   water
jumps from their mouths.
Jaws of lions are snarling   water
through green teeth over chins of moss.
Dolphins toss jets of   water
from open snouts
to an upper theatre of   water.
Children are riding swans and   water
coils from the S-shaped necks and spills
in flat foils from pincered bills.
A solemn curly headed bull
puts out a swollen tongue of   water.
Cupids naked are making   water
into a font that never is full.
A goddess is driving a chariot through   water.
Her reins and whips are tight white   water.
Bronze hooves of horses wrangle with   water.
Marble faces half hidden in leaves.
Faces whose hair is leaves and grapes
of stone are peering from living leaves.
Faces with mossy lips unlocked
always uttering   water.
Water
wearing their features blank
their ears deaf, their eyes mad
or patient or blind or astonished at   water
always uttered out of their mouths.

WORD POEMS

TO MAKE A PLAY

To make a play
is to make people,
to make people do
what you say;

to make real people
do and say
what you make;
to make people make

what you say real;
to make real
people make up
and do what you

make up. What you
make makes people
come and see
what people do

and say, and then
go away and do
what they see—
and see what

they do. Real
people do and say,
and you see and
make up people;

people come to see
what you do.
They see what *they*
do, and they

may go away undone.
You can make
people, or you
can unmake. You

can do or you
can undo. People
you make up make up
and make people;

people come to
see—to see
themselves real,
and they go away

and do what you
say—as if they
were made up,
and wore makeup.

To make a play
is to make
people; to make
people make

themselves; to
make people
make themselves
new. So real.

THE WATCH

When I
took my
watch to the watchfixer I
felt privileged but also pained to watch the operation. He
had long fingernails and a voluntary squint. He
fixed a magnifying cup over his
squint eye. He
undressed my
watch. I
watched him
split her
in three layers and lay her
middle—a quivering viscera—in a circle on a little plinth. He
shoved shirtsleeves up and leaned like an ogre over my
naked watch. With critical pincers he
poked and stirred. He
lifted out little private things with a magnet too tiny for me
to watch almost. "Watch out!" I
almost said. His
eye watched, enlarged, the secrets of my
watch, and I
watched anxiously. Because what if he
touched her
ticker too rough, and she
gave up the ghost out of pure fright? Or put her
things back backwards so she'd
run backwards after this? Or he
might lose a minuscule part, connected to her
exquisite heart, and mix her
up, instead of fix her.

And all the time,
all the time-
pieces on the walls, on the shelves, told the time,
told the time
in swishes and ticks
swishes and ticks,
and seemed to be gloating, as they watched and told. I
felt faint, I
was about to lose my
breath—my
ticker going lickety-split—when watchfixer clipped her
three slices together with a gleam and two flicks of his
tools like chopsticks. He
spat out his
eye, lifted her
high, gave her
a twist, set her
hands right, and laid her
little face, quite as usual, in its place on my
wrist.

ANALYSIS OF BASEBALL

It's about
the ball,
the bat,
and the mitt.
Ball hits
bat, or it
hits mitt.
Bat doesn't
hit ball, bat
meets it.
Ball bounces
off bat, flies
air, or thuds
ground (dud)
or it
fits mitt.

Bat waits
for ball
to mate.
Ball hates
to take bat's
bait. Ball
flirts, bat's
late, don't
keep the date.
Ball goes in
(thwack) to mitt,
and goes out
(thwack) back
to mitt.

Ball fits
mitt, but
not all
the time.
Sometimes
ball gets hit
(pow) when bat
meets it,
and sails
to a place
where mitt
has to quit
in disgrace.
That's about
the bases
loaded,
about 40,000
fans exploded.

It's about
the ball,
the bat,
the mitt,
the bases
and the fans.
It's done
on a diamond,
and for fun.
It's about
home, and it's
about run.

THE PREGNANT DREAM

I had a   dream in which I had a
dream,
and in my   dream I told you,
"Listen, I will tell you my
dream." And I began to tell you. And
you told me, "I haven't time to   listen while you tell your
dream."

Then in my   dream I
dreamed I began to
forget my
dream.
And I   forgot my
dream.
And I began to tell you,   "Listen, I have
forgot my
dream."
And now I tell you: "Listen while I tell you my
dream, a
dream
in which I   dreamed I
forgot my
dream,"
and I begin to tell you: "In my   dream you told me, 'I haven't time to
listen.' "

And you tell me: "You   dreamed I wouldn't
listen to a
dream that you
forgot?
I haven't time to   listen to
forgotten
dreams."
"But I haven't   forgot I
dreamed," I tell you,
"a   dream in which I told you,
'Listen, I have
forgot,' and you told me, 'I haven't time.' "
"I haven't time," you tell me.

And now I begin to   forget that I
                       forgot what I began to tell you in my
                       dream.
        And I tell you,   "Listen,
                       listen, I begin to
                       forget."

MAsterMANANiMAl

ANiMAte MANANiMAl MAttress of Nerves
MANipulAtor Motor ANd Motive MAker
MAMMAliAN MAtrix MAt of rivers red
MortAl MANic Morsel Mover shAker

MAteriAl-MAster MAsticAtor oxygeN-eAter
MouNtAiN-MouNter MApper peNetrAtor
iN MoNster MetAl MANtle of the Air
MAssive wAter-surgeoN prestidigitAtor

MAchiNist MAsoN MesoN-Mixer MArble-heAver
coiNer cArver cities-idols-AtoMs-sMAsher
electric lever Metric AlcheMist
MeNtAl AMAzer igNorANt iNcubAtor

cANNibAl AutoMANANiMAl cAllous cAlculAtor
Milky MAgNetic MAN iNNoceNt iNNovAtor
MAlleAble MAMMAl MercuriAl ANd MAteriAl
MAster ANiMAl ANd ANiMA etheriAl

M=55
A=77
N=42

COLOR AND
SOUND POEMS

THE BLINDMAN

The blindman placed
a tulip on his tongue for purple's taste.
Cheek to grass, his green

was rough excitement's sheen
of little whips.
In water to his lips

he named the sea blue and white,
the basin of his tears and fallen beads of sight.
He said: This scarf is red;

I feel the vectors to its thread
that dance down from the sun. I know
the seven fragrances of the rainbow.

I have caressed
the orange hair of flames. Pressed
to my ear,

a pomegranate lets me hear
crimson's flute.
Trumpets tell me yellow. Only ebony is mute.

FLAG OF SUMMER

Sky and sea and sand,
fabric of the day.
The eye compares each band.

Parallels of color on bare
canvas of time-by-the-sea.
Linen-clean the air.

Tan of the burlap
beach scuffed with prints
of bathers. Green and dapple,

the serpentine swipe
of the sea unraveling
a ragged crepe

on the shore. Heavy satin
far out, the coil,
darkening, flattens

to the sky's rim.
There a gauze screen,
saturate-blue, shimmers.

Blue and green and tan,
the fabric changes hues
by brush of light or rain:

sky's violet bar
leans over flinty waves
opaque as the shore's

opaline grains; sea silvers,
clouds fade to platinum,
the sand-mat ripples

with greenish tints
of snakeskin, or drying,
whitens to tent-cloth

spread in the sun. These bands,
primary in their dimensions,
elements, textures, strands:

the flag of summer,
emblem of ease, triple-striped,
each day salutes the swimmer.

COLORS WITHOUT OBJECTS

Colors without objects—colors alone—
wriggle in the tray of my eye,

incubated under the great flat lamp
of the sun:

bodiless blue, little razor-streak,
yellow melting like a firework petal,

double purple yo-yo
in a broth of murky gold.

Sharp green squints I have never seen
minnow-dive the instant they're alive;

bulb-reds with flickering cilia
dilate, but then implode

to discs of impish scotomata
that flee into the void;

weird orange slats of hot thought
about to make a basket—but

there is no material here—they slim
to a snow of needles, are erased.

Now a mottling takes place.
All colors fix chromosomic links

that dexterously mix,
flip, exchange their aerial ladders.

Such stunts of speed and metamorphosis
breed impermanent, objectless acts,

a thick, a brilliant bacteria—
but most do not survive.

I wait for a few iridium specks of idea
to thrive in the culture of my eye.

RAIN AT WILDWOOD

The rain fell like grass growing
upside down in the dark,
at first thin shoots,
short, crisp, far apart,

but, roots in the clouds,
a thick mat grew
quick, loquacious, lachrymose blades
blunt on the tent top.

The grass beneath ticked,
trickled, tickled like rain
all night, inchwormed
under our ears,

its flat liquid tips slipping
east with the slope.
Various tin plates
and cups and a bucket filled

up outside,
played, plinked, plicked,
plopped till guttural.
The raccoon's prowl was almost

silent in the trash,
soggy everything but eggshells.
No owl called.
Waking at first light

the birds were blurred,
notes and dyes of jay and towhee
guaranteed to bleed.
And no bluing in the sky.

In the inverted V
of the tent flaps
muddy sheets of morning
slumped among the trunks,

but the pin oaks' veridian
dripping raggedy leaves
on the wood's floor released
tangy dews and ozones.

HEARING THE WIND AT NIGHT

I heard the wind coming,
transferred from tree to tree.
I heard the leaves
swish, wishing to be free

to come with the wind, yet wanting to stay
with the boughs like sleeves.
The wind was a green ghost.
Possessed of tearing breath

the body of each tree
whined, a whipping post,
then straightened and resumed
its vegetable oath.

I heard the wind going,
and it went wild.
Somewhere the forest threw itself
into tantrum like a child.

I heard the trees tossing
in punishment or grief,
then sighing, and soughing,
soothing themselves to sleep.

STONE GULLETS

Stone Gullets among   Inrush   Feed   Backsuck and

The boulders swallow   Outburst   Huge engorgements   Swallow

In gulps the sea   Tide crams jagged   Smacks snorts chuckups   Follow

In urgent thirst   Jaws the hollow   Insurge   Hollow

Gushing evacuations follow   Jetty it must   Outpush   Greed

ELECTRONIC SOUND

A pebble swells to a boulder at low speed.
                    At $7\frac{1}{2}$ *ips* a hiss is a hurricane.
                                   The basin drain
is Charybdis sucking
                         a clipper down, the ship
                                    a paperclip
whirling. Or gargle, brush your teeth, hear
                    a winded horse's esophagus lurch
                         on playback at 15/16. Perch
a quarter on edge on a plate, spin:
                    a locomotive's wheel is wrenched loose,
               wobbles down the line to slam the caboose,
keeps on snicking over the ties
                         till it teeters on the embankment,
                              bowls down a cement
ramp, meanders onto the turnpike
                              and into a junkhole
                    of scrapped cars. Ceasing to roll,
it shimmies, falters...
                         Sudden inertia causes
                                        pause.
Then a round of echoes
                         descending, a minor yammer
as when a triangle's nicked by the slimmest hammer.

CREATURE POEMS

A PAIR

A he
and she,
prowed upstream,
soot-brown
necks,
bills the green
of spring
asparagus,

heads
proud figure-
heads for the boat-
bodies, smooth
hulls on feathered　　　　the two,
water,　　　　browed with light,
steer ashore,
rise; four
web-
paddles pigeon-
toe it
to the reeds;

he
walks first,
proud, prowed
as when light-
browed, swimming,
he leads.

CAMOUFLEUR

Walked in the swamp   His cheek vermilion
          A dazzling prince
     Neck-band white   Cape he trailed
          Metallic mottled
Over rain-rotted leaves   Wet mud reflected
          Waded olive water
     His opulent gear   Pillars of the reeds
          Parted the strawgold
          Brilliance   Made him disappear

GEOMETRID

Writhes, rides down
on his own spit,
lets breeze twist

him so he chins,
humps, reels up it,
munching back

the vomit string.
Some drools
round his neck.

Arched into a staple
now, high on green
oak leaf he punctures

for food, what
was the point
of his act? Not

to spangle the air,
or show me his trick.
Breeze broke

his suck,
so he spit
a fraction of self's

length forth, bled
colorless from within,
to catch a balance,

glide to a knot
made with his own mouth.
Ruminant

while climbing, got
back better than bitten
leaf. Breeze

that threw
him snagged him
to a new.

CATBIRD IN REDBUD

Catbird in the redbud this morning.
No cat could
mimic that rackety cadenza he's making.
And it's not red,
the trapeze he's swaying on.
After last night's freeze,
redbud's violet-pink, twinkled on
by the sun. That bird's
red, though, under the tail
he wags, up sharply, like a wren.

The uncut lawn hides blue
violets with star-gold eyes on the longest
stems I've ever seen. Going to
empty the garbage, I simply have
to pick some,
reaching to the root of green,
getting my fist dewy, happening
to tear up a dandelion, too.

Lilac, hazy blue—
violet, nods buds over the alley
fence, and (like a horse with a yen
for something fresh for breakfast)
I put my nose into a fragrant
pompom, bite off some, and chew.

Unconscious
came a beauty to my
wrist
and stopped my pencil,
merged its shadow profile with
my hand's ghost
on the page:
Red Spotted Purple or else Mourning
Cloak,
paired thin as paper wings, near black,
were edged on the seam side poppy orange,
as were its spots.

UNCONSCIOUS

CAME A BEAUTY

I sat arrested, for its soot haired
body's worm
shone in the sun.
It bent its tongue long as
a leg
black on my skin
and clung without my
feeling,
while its tomb stained
duplicate parts of
a window opened.
And then I
moved.

REDUNDANT JOURNEY

I'll rest here in the bend of my tail
said the python having traveled
his own length
beginning with his squared snout
laid beside his neck
O where does the neck
end and the chest begin
O where does the stomach
end and the loins begin
O where are the arms and legs
Now I'll travel between myself
said the python lifting his snout
and his blue eyes saw lead-gray
frames like windows on his hide
the glisten of himself the chill
pattern on each side
of himself and as his head slept
between the middles of himself
the end of his outer self still crept
The python reared his neck and yawned
his tongue was twins his mucous membrane
purple pink hibiscus sticky
He came to a cul de sac in the lane
of the center of his length
his low snout
trapped between twin windowed
creeping hills of himself
and no way out
I'll travel upon myself said the python
lifting his chin to a hill
of his inner length and while
his neck crossed one half of his
stomach his chest crossed his
loins while his tail lay still
But then he thought
I feel uncomfortable in
this upright knot
and he lowered his chin
from the shelf of himself
and tucked his snout in
How get away from myself said
the python beside himself
traveling his own side
How recognize myself as just myself
instead of a labyrinth I must travel
over and over stupified
His snout came to the end
of himself again to the final leaden bend
of himself
Said the python to his tail
Let's both rest till all
the double windowed middle maze
of ourself
gets through crawling

MOTHERHOOD

She sat on a shelf,
her breasts two bellies
on her poked-out belly,
on which the navel looked
like a sucked-in-mouth—
her knees bent and apart,
her long left arm raised,
with the large hand knuckled
to a bar in the ceiling—
her right hand clamping
the skinny infant to her chest—
its round, pale, new,
soft muzzle hunting
in the brown hair for a nipple,
its splayed, tiny hand picking
at her naked, dirty ear.
Twisting its little neck,
with tortured, ecstatic eyes
the size of lentils, it looked
into her severe, close-set,
solemn eyes, that beneath bald
eyelids glared—dull lights
in sockets of leather.

She twitched some chin-hairs,
with pain or pleasure,
as the baby-mouth found and
yanked at her nipple;
its pink-nailed, jointless
fingers, wandering her face,
tangled in the tufts
of her cliffy brows.
She brought her big
hand down from the bar—
with pretended exasperation
unfastened the little hand,
and locked it within her palm—
while her right hand,
with snag-nailed forefinger

and short, sharp thumb, raked
the new orange hair
of the infant's skinny flank—
and found a louse,
which she lipped, and
thoughtfully crisped
between broad teeth.
She wrinkled appreciative
nostrils which, without a nose,
stood open—damp, holes
above the poke of her mouth.

She licked her lips, flicked
her leather eyelids—
then, suddenly flung
up both arms and grabbed
the bars overhead.
The baby's scrabbly fingers
instantly caught the hair—
as if there were metal rings there—
in her long, stretched armpits.
And, as she stately swung,
and then proudly, more swiftly
slung herself from corner
to corner of her cell—
arms longer than her round
body, short knees bent—
her little wild-haired,
poke-mouthed infant hung,
like some sort of trophy,
or decoration, or shaggy medal—
shaped like herself—but new,
clean, soft and shining
on her chest.

A BIRD'S LIFE

Is every day a separate life to a bird?
Else why,
as dawn finds the slit lid of starling- or sparrow-eye,
spurts that mad bouquet from agape bills?
Streamered, corkscrew, soprano tendrils
riot in the garden—
incredulous ejaculations at the first pinches
of birth. Tiny winches
are tightened, then hysterically jerked loose.
There is produced
a bright geyser of metal-petaled sound
that, shredding, rubs its filings into my sleep.

As the sun, Herself, bulges from a crack in the cloud-shell,
a clamp is applied to every peep—
a paralysis of awe, as they are ovened
under the feathers of Mother Light—
a stun
of silence. Then they revert
to usual.

When the sun
is higher, only a blurt
of chitters, here and there,
from the sparrows—
sassy whistles, sarcastic barks from the starlings.
By noon they're into middle age
and the stodgy business of generation.

Evening, though, leaks
elegy from a few pathetic beaks.
Chirks of single-syllable despair
that the sky is empty and their
flit-lives almost done.
Their death is the death of light.
Do they lack memory, and so
not know
that the Hen
of the sun
will hatch them again
next morning?

NEWS FROM THE CABIN

1

Hairy was here.
He hung on a sumac seed pod.
Part of his double tail hugged the crimson
 scrotum under cockscomb leaves—
 or call it blushing lobster claw, that swatch—
 a toothy match to Hairy's red skullpatch.
Cried *peek!* Beaked it—chiselled the drupe.
His nostril I saw, slit in a slate whistle.
White-black dominoes clicked in his wings.
Bunched beneath the dangle he heckled with holes,
 bellysack soft, eye a brad, a red-flecked
 mallet his ball-peen head, his neck its haft.

2

Scurry was here.
He sat up like a six-inch bear,
 rocked on the porch with me;
 brought his own chair, his chow-haired tail.
Ate a cherry I threw.
Furry paunch, birchbark-snowy, pinecone-brown back
 a jacket with sleeves to the digits.
Sat put, pert, neat, in his suit and his seat, for a minute,
 a frown between snub ears—bulb-eyed head
 toward me sideways, chewed.
Rocked, squeaked. Stored the stone in his cheek.
Finished, fell to all fours, a little roan couch;
 flurried paws loped him off, prone-bodied,
 tail turned torch, sail, scarf.

3

Then, Slicker was here.
Dipped down, cobalt and turquoise brushes
   fresh as paint. Gripped a pine-tassle,
   folded his flaunts, parted his pointed nib, and scrawled
   jeeah! on the air.
Japanned so smooth, his head-peak and all his shaft:
   harsh taunts from that dovey shape, soft tints—
   nape and chin black-splintered, quilltips white-lashed.
Javelin-bird, he slurred his color,
   left his ink-bold word here; flashed off.
Morning prints his corvine noise elsewhere,
   while that green toss still quivers with his equipoise.

4

And Supple was here.
Lives nearby at the stump.
Trickled out from under, when the sun struck there.
Mud-and-silver-licked, his length—a single spastic muscle—
   slid over stones and twigs to a snuggle of roots, and hid.
I followed that elastic: loose
   unicolored knot, a noose he made as if unconscious.
Until my shadow touched him: half his curd
   shuddered, the rest lay chill.
I stirred: the ribbon raised a loop;
   its end stretched, then cringed like an udder;
   a bifid tongue, his only rapid, whirred
   in the vent; vertical pupils lit his hood.
That part, a groping finger, hinged, stayed upright.
Indicated what? That I stood
   in his light? I left the spot.

THE WONDERFUL PEN

I invented a wonderful pen. Not a typewriter...I wanted to use
just one hand, the right. With my hand always bent, the ink tube
a vein in my wrist, fixed between finger and thumb the pen wrote
as fast as I could feel. It chose all the right words for my feelings.
But then, my feelings ran out through the pen. It went dry. I had
a book of wonderful feelings, but my right hand was paralyzed.
I threw away the pen.

I invented a dream camera: a box, with a visor or mask...like a
stereopticon. When I awoke, I could view, and review, my dreams,
entire, in their depth. Events, visions, symbols, colors without
names, dazzled, obsessed me. They scalded my sight. I threw
away the camera. I had a moving picture of my wonderful dreams,
but I was blind.

So, with my left hand I wrote. I had been lazy so long...
The letters went backwards across the page. Sometimes they went
upside down: a "q" for a "b," a "d" for a "p," or an "n" for a "u,"
an "m" for a "w." And it got worse. Now, since I can't read, or
see, not even the mirror can tell me, what I mean by the first
line by the time I've written the last line. But my feelings
are back, and my dreams...

What I write is so hard to write. It must be hard to read.
So slow...So swift my mind, so stupid my pen. I think I'll invent
a typewriter...For the left hand, and no eyes. No! I throw
away the thought. But I have a wonderful mind: Inventive. It is
for you to find. Read *me*. Read my mind.

INDEX OF TITLES

After the Flight of Ranger 7, 52
Analysis of Baseball, 81
At Breakfast, 2
At Truro, 68

Beginning to Squall, 71
Bird's Life, A, 104
Blindman, The, 86
Boy Looking at Big David, A, 46
By Morning, 5

Camoufleur, 97
Cardinal Ideograms, 11
Cat and the Weather, 21
Catbird in Redbud, 99
Centaur, The, 47
Charm Box, The, 30
Cloud-Mobile, The, 41
Colors Without Objects, 89

Drawing the Cat, 22

Electronic Sound, 94
Evolution, 45
Extremity, An, 10

Feel Like a Bird, 28
First Walk on the Moon, 55
Flag of Summer, 87
Forest, 26
Fountain Piece, 27
Fountains of Aix, 75

Geometrid, 98
Green Red Brown and White, 38

Hearing the Wind at Night, 92
Her Management, 17
His Secret, 24
How Everything Happens (Based on a Study of the Wave), 72
Hypnotist, 7

Japanese Breakfast, 15

Living Tenderly, 6

MAsterMANANiMAl, 84
Motherhood, 102

News from the Cabin, 105

Of Rounds, 63
Orbiter 5 Shows How Earth Looks from the Moon, 54
Out of the Sea, Early, 69
Over the Field, 59

Pair, A, 96
Pregnant Dream, The, 82

Question, 42

Rain at Wildwood, 90
Redundant Journey, 101

Seven Natural Songs, 14
Sleeping Overnight on the Shore, 61
Southbound on the Freeway, 13
Stick, The, 73
Stone Gullets, 93
Surface, The, 16

Three Jet Planes, 58
3 Models of the Universe, 44
Tide at Long Point, The, 33
To Make a Play, 78

Unconscious Came a Beauty, 100

Waiting for *It*, 20
Waking from a Nap on the Beach, 70
Was Worm, 4
Watch, The, 79
Water Picture, 40
Wave and the Dune, The, 34
Wave the Flame the Cloud and the Leopard Speak to the Mind, The, 43
When You Lie Down, the Sea Stands Up, 35
Whiteness, i
Window in the Tail, 60
Wonderful Pen, The 109
Woods at Night, The, 32
Word "Beautiful," The, 39

Yellow Circle, A, 8

INDEX OF FIRST LINES

A bird, 27
A bloody, 69
Above my face is a map, 41
A Buoy like a man in a red sou'wester, 71
A green, 8
A he, 96
Ahead, the sun's face in a flaring hood, 55
A mouth. Can blow or breathe, 11
ANiMAte MANANiMAl MAttress of Nerves, 84
A pebble swells to a boulder at low speed, 94
As if the knob, 30
At moment X, 44
A tourist came in from Orbitville, 13
Awoke and stretched in all the bodies, 14

Beards of water, 75
Bit an apple on its red, 38
Body my house, 42

Catbird in the redbud this morning, 99
Cat takes a look at the weather, 21
Colors without objects—colors alone, 89

Earth turns, 61

Feel like A Bird, 28
First I saw the surface, 16

Hairy was here, 105
His lair framed beneath the clock, 7

I had a dream in which I had a, 82
I heard the wind coming, 92
I invented a wonderful pen, 109
I'll rest here in the bend of my tail, 101
I'm touching his toe, 46
In the pond in the park, 40
Is every day a separate life to a bird, 104
I took my cat apart, 24
It's about, 81

Long, glossy caterpillar, 39

Makes a platform for himself, 22
Moon, 63
Moon, old fossil, 52
My body a rounded stone, 6
My cat jumps to the window sill, 20

Nap of cloud, as thick as stuffing, 60
Not quite, 2

Roused from napping in my lap, 10

She does not place, relate, or name, 17
She sat on a shelf, 102
Sky and sea and sand, 87
Some for everyone, 5
Sounds like big, 70
Stone gullets, 93

The binocular owl, 32
The blindman placed, 86
The pines, aggressive as erect tails of cats, 26
The rain fell like grass growing, 90
The sea comes up and the sun goes over, 33
The sea is unfolding scrolls, 68
The stick is subject to the waves. The waves are subject to, 73
The stone, 45
The summer that I was ten, 47
The table of the pool is set, 15
The wave-shaped dune is still, 34
There's a woman in the earth, sitting on, 54
They have, 59
Thick twisted cables, 35
Three jet planes skip above the roofs, 58
To make a play, 78

Unconscious, 100

Walked in the swamp, 97
Was worm, 4
Watch and watch and follow me, 43
What is whiter, i
When I, 79
When nothing is happening, 72
Writhes, rides down, 98

ABOUT THE AUTHOR

May Swenson was born in Logan, Utah, in 1913. After graduating from college, she moved to New York City and worked at different times as an author's assistant, secretary, and manuscript reader—but she devoted every spare moment to writing poetry. Her poems appeared in many newspapers and magazines and were published in ten collections during her lifetime, seven of which were nominated for the National Book Award. May Swenson earned a multitude of fellowships and awards, including Rockefeller and Guggenheim Fellowships, the Bollingen Prize, and a MacArthur Fellowship. She wrote an experimental play, *The Floor*, which was produced at the American Place Theater. May Swenson read and was poet-in-residence at many colleges and universities throughout the country. Her poems and prose have been published in more than one hundred anthologies and her poetry has been translated into French, Spanish, German, Italian, Danish, and Swedish. May Swenson died in 1989 at the age of 76. In 1991, *The Love Poems of May Swenson* was published posthumously.